YAS

W9-BAZ-937

# THE COUNTRYSIDE

Life in the Renaissance

# THE COUNTRYSIDE

KATHRYN HINDS

**BENCHMARK BOOKS**

MARSHALL CAVENDISH
NEW YORK

# To the Lumpkin Library Ladies

Grateful acknowledgment is made to Monica Chojnacka, Associate Professor of History, University of Georgia, for her generous assistance in reading the manuscript.

Benchmark Books
Marshall Cavendish
99 White Plains Road
Tarrytown, New York 10591-9001
www.marshallcavendish.com

**Library of Congress Cataloging-in-Publication Data**

Hinds, Kathryn, 1962-

The countryside / by Kathryn Hinds.

p. cm. — (Life in the Renaissance)

Includes bibliographical references and index.

Summary: Describes the social and economic structure of country life during the Renaissance, from about 1400–1600, and the role of the peasants, villagers, and landowners in the shaping of European civilization.

ISBN 0-7614-1677-3

1. Renaissance—Juvenile literature. 2. Country life—Europe—History—To 1500—Juvenile literature. 3. Country life—Europe—History—16th century—Juvenile literature. 4. Europe—Social life and customs—Juvenile literature. [1. Renaissance. 2. Country life—Europe—History—To 1500. 3. Country life—Europe—History—16th century.] I. Title. II. Series.

CB367.H56 2003

940.2'1'09734—dc21

2003001449

Art Research: Rose Corbett Gordon, Mystic CT

Cover: Erich Lessing/Art Resource, NY

Page 1: Bibliotheque de l'Arsenal/Archives Charmet/Bridgeman Art Library; pages 2, 13, 21, 24, 29 & 31: Scala/Art Resource, NY; page 10: Galleria degli Uffizi, Florence/Bridgeman Art Library; pages 15, 26, 42, 43, 53 & 69: The Pierpont Morgan Library/Art Resource, NY; pages 17, 49, 79: Réunion des Musées Nationaux/Art Resource, NY; page 33: The Barnes Foundation, Merion, Pennsylvania/Bridgeman Art Library; page 35: Art Resource, NY; pages 40 & 51: Alinari/Art Resource, NY; page 46: By Courtesy of the National Portrait Gallery, London; pages 55, 68 & 73: Erich Lessing/Art Resource, NY; page 58: Louvre, Paris/Giraudon-Bridgeman Art Library; page 60: Offentliche Kunstsammlung, Basel, Switzerland/Giraudon-Bridgeman Art Library; page 62: Johnny van Haeften Gallery, London/Bridgeman Art Library; page 64: Fine Arts Photographic Library, London/Art Resource, NY; page 74: Fitzwilliam Museum, University of Cambridge, UK/Bridgeman Art Library; page 77: British Library, London/Bridgeman Art Library; page 81: Private Collection/Bridgeman Art Library; page 82: Foto Marburg/Art Resource, NY.

Printed in China

135642

*cover:* Peasants bring farm products to sell in a town market.

*half title page:* A woman with a winnowing basket, used to separate kernels of wheat from the chaff after harvesting.

*title page:* A young woman spins as a companion looks on. The older woman in front of them appears to be giving instructions to servants.

# CONTENTS

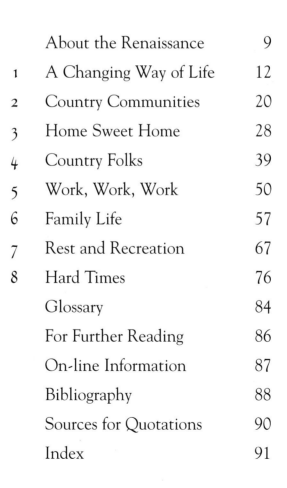

# THE COUNTRYSIDE

# ABOUT THE RENAISSANCE

When we talk about the Renaissance, we generally mean the period of western European history from roughly 1400 to 1600. The Renaissance can also be understood as a cultural movement in which art, literature, music, philosophy, and education shared in certain trends and influences. This movement had its origins in fourteenth-century Florence, Italy. Here the great writer Francesco Petrarca, or Petrarch, promoted the idea of a rebirth of the literature and learning of ancient Greece and Rome—*renaissance* means "rebirth."

This notion gradually spread throughout Italy and much of the rest of western Europe. As it did, people also grew interested in giving new life to Greek and Roman styles of art and architecture. In the process of rediscovering ancient culture and adapting it to the times, Renaissance people began to create unique cultures of their own. Many Europeans developed a great love of beauty, art, and learning for their own sake.

Some Renaissance thinkers felt that they were living at the dawn of a magnificent new era, leaving behind a time they considered "the dark ages." They believed that they would not only revive the glories of the ancient world, but surpass them. This belief seemed to be confirmed as new artistic techniques, architectural styles, philosophies, and educational practices caught on all over Europe. Historians now realize, however, that the seeds of these magnificent achievements were already present in medieval Europe. But although the

*One of the Renaissance's greatest artists was Raphael. In this portrait of a young nobleman, Raphael brilliantly depicts the gentleman's rich clothing and furs, a clear indication of his high status.*

Renaissance did not make a total break with the past, three momentous changes occurred during this period that definitely paved the way to the future.

First was the invention of movable type and the printing press. Two German goldsmiths, Johannes Gutenberg and Johann Fust, invented movable type in 1446–1448. Then, between 1450 and 1455 Gutenberg used the world's first printing press to produce the world's first printed book, the famous Gutenberg Bible. Before this, all books had been written out and produced entirely by hand. They were therefore expensive and fairly rare. Since most people could not afford to own books, most people did not learn how to read. With the printing press, books—and the ideas and stories contained in them—became much more widely available.

Second, the Renaissance was a period when Europeans made many voyages of exploration. Explorers originally sought new and better routes to Asia, the source of silk, spices, and other goods that brought high prices in European markets. In 1492 the Italian explorer Christopher Columbus landed on the island of Hispaniola in the Caribbean. At first it was thought that this land was part of Asia. By 1500 it was clear that Columbus had reached a continent whose existence had been previously unknown to most Europeans. It was a true turning point in world history.

The third great change for western Europe was the Protestant Reformation. During the Middle Ages, western Europe had been united by one Church, headquartered in the ancient Italian city of Rome. In 1517 a monk named Martin Luther nailed a list of protests to a German cathedral door. Luther hoped to reform the Catholic Church, to purify it and rid it of corrupt practices. Instead, his action sparked the beginning of a new religious movement. Now there were many conflicting ideas about what it meant to be a Christian.

Renaissance people had many of the same joys and sorrows, hopes and fears that we do. They were poised at the beginning of the modern age, but still their world was very different from ours. Forget about telephones, computers, cars, and televisions, and step back into a time when printed books were a wonderful new thing. Let the Renaissance come alive. . . .

# One

# A CHANGING WAY OF LIFE

During the time we call the Renaissance, 80 to 90 percent of Europeans lived in the country and worked at farming and related jobs. In many ways, their lives went on just as they had done for centuries. The average peasant did not care much about the rebirth of ancient learning or new artistic techniques. Everyday concerns about crops, livestock, and the weather were more important.

Still, country dwellers were more and more affected by the historic changes taking place. For instance, by the 1500s printing presses were turning out inexpensive pamphlets and broadsides. These could include anything from ballads and popular stories to news of overseas discoveries to religious tracts. Traveling peddlers sold these publications at country fairs and the like. Most places had at least one literate person who was willing to read them aloud to other villagers. In many areas village schools were opened, and more country children learned to read than ever before. In England, for example, by 1600 roughly one-third of the nation's males were able to read.

*A wealthy couple* (in black, on the right) *pay a charitable visit to a busy farmhouse where several generations of a family are living and working together.*

The Reformation was another cause of increasing literacy. The version of the Bible used by the Catholic Church was in Latin, which most people did not understand. Protestants believed that the Bible should be translated into the language spoken by people in their everyday lives so that every Christian could read the Bible for themselves. Thanks to the printing press and the Reformers, affordable Bibles began to appear in German, French, English, and other languages. This gave ordinary people, especially in Protestant communities, another strong reason to learn to read. Reformers often set up schools to teach them.

Some of the Reformation's effects were less beneficial. The new religious movement sparked wars and other violence that often harmed country communities. In territories that became Protestant, convents and monasteries were closed down. Many peasant communities had depended on these institutions not only for religious guidance but also for medical care, poor relief, and other social services. In addition, numerous country families had rented their land from some of these religious communities for generations. Now convent and monastery lands were taken over by the government or put up for sale.

Farmers who were already fairly prosperous were able to increase their holdings and enjoy a rising standard of living. The average peasant, however, could not afford to buy much land, so wealthy nobles, merchants, lawyers, and the like acquired more and more property. These landowners rented out parcels of land, but there was only a limited amount available to tenants, and rents were high. In addition, birth rates were increasing and the population was growing. The Renaissance "baby boom" led to lower wages and higher prices for food, land, and other resources. Even as life improved for "the middling sort," for poor peasants the Renaissance was a very hard time indeed.

## COUNTRY AND CITY

Numerous people left the countryside and moved to the city to try to improve their lives. Others traveled to nearby towns fairly often to attend fairs and markets. Most Renaissance cities had a very close relationship with the surrounding countryside. Many townspeople even left their homes every workday to labor on farms outside the city walls.

Urban areas depended on the country for basic food supplies. Hundreds of peasants might come to a city on market day, bringing fruits, vegetables, eggs, cheeses, and other farm products to sell. Grain was brought into cities by the cartload, cattle were driven to the butchers, and wool was delivered to cloth manufacturers. In return for such products, peasants

A well-off townsman buys a bull from a peasant (in blue jacket), who seems reluctant to let the animal go for just the few coins he's been handed.

received money to pay their rent or perhaps to buy a few things that they could not make or grow themselves.

Many cities ruled the country areas around them. If peasants had legal problems, they had to go into the city to appear in court, pay fines, and so on. For example, Nuremberg, Germany, had a Peasant Court, which was held for three hours every Saturday afternoon. One of Nuremberg's legal advisers explained, "This Peasant Court has jurisdiction over all controversies arising among the rural people of our Territory." In a few places, peasants who owned their own land could choose someone to represent their interests to the local town government. However, this was rare, and country people usually had little say about the laws, taxes, and government decisions that affected them.

# LANDLORDS AND THEIR DEMANDS

There were many different arrangements between peasants and landowners. In much of eastern Europe, most sixteenth-century peasants were serfs, tied to a particular estate or piece of land. Eastern Europe did not have many well developed urban centers, but it did have large areas where grain and livestock could be raised. These products and other raw materials were in high demand in western Europe. Wealthy nobles became even wealthier by meeting that demand. They bought up huge plots of land and gradually required more payments and services from the peasants living on the land. In Poland, for example, laws in 1520 ordered peasants to work one day a week for their lords. Around 1550 the requirement changed to three days a week, and by 1600 it was six days a week.

Serfdom had been common in much of western Europe during the Middle Ages. It still existed in places, but by the 1400s large numbers of serfs had been able to buy their freedom. Freedom meant that peasants were no longer bound to a lord's land. They were free to move from one village to another, and they could buy and sell land of their own. They were free, too, from the many fees that serfs were required to pay their lords. Nevertheless, tenant farmers—those who rented their land—had some obligations. Along with paying rent, they might have to work a few days a year for the landlord or supply him with various farm products. Farmers were often expected to sell most of their produce to the landlord at low prices. The landlord would then resell the grain, wool, and so on at much higher prices.

In many places landlords owned all of a community's mills, ovens, fish ponds, and woods. A peasant who wanted to grind grain, bake bread, catch fish, or gather firewood had to pay the landlord a fee to do so. Landlords usually allowed no one except themselves and their friends to hunt in the woods they owned. Anyone else caught hunting was guilty of poaching, a crime that was seriously punished. The landlord was often responsible for hearing and judging legal cases on his lands, and kept any fines that had to be paid by offenders.

A baker tends to bread that's still in the oven while customers look over the loaves on the counter. In some places villagers baked their bread themselves, in community ovens owned by a lord. Other villages had bakeries, like this one, where people could buy bread from the local baker.

# A Free Village

In the village of Artigat in southern France, as in some other villages, all of the landowners were peasants. Poorer peasants might pay rents to richer ones, but no one owed fees or services to any noble landlord. The people of Artigat were very proud of their freedom, especially since the village just upriver had a lord, and a castle from which he could control the peasants who worked his lands.

In a free village like Artigat, all local affairs were in the hands of the villagers themselves. Larger matters were subject only to the king of France and his representatives. For Artigat, the lowest ranking of the king's agents was his judge in the town of Rieux, several hours away. If a matter had to go to a higher authority, it went to the seneschal, or steward, of Toulouse, the leading city in the region. After that, an appeal could be made to the parliament of Toulouse, but it was a rare case that had to be dealt with at such a high level.

Artigat's local government was headed by three or four consuls, leading villagers chosen yearly by an assembly of the community's men. The judge of Rieux had to approve their selection, but that was all. The consuls, who wore red and white hoods as their badge of office, decided such matters as when to start the winter harvest and how to distribute the common lands. They gave judgments on disturbance of the peace, use of false weights and measures, minor assaults, and similar cases. When a peasant died without heirs, the consuls handled the auction of his goods. If an orphan needed to be assigned a guardian, the consuls took care of that, too. They often called an assembly of all the village's men to take part in decision making—but women were not summoned to join the assembly unless the consuls were proclaiming a law or order for all the village.

Another way for landlords to make money from the peasantry was by charging tolls for using roads or bridges on their property. Even freeholders, peasants who owned their own land, would have to pay these fees when they used toll roads and bridges. Freeholders, tenant farmers, and landlords alike all had to pay taxes to the government and tithes to the church. In some areas, roughly 40 percent of a peasant's income went just for taxes, tithes, and various fees.

# Two

# COUNTRY COMMUNITIES

P easant communities differed from each other largely according to how easy the land was to farm. Mountainous areas, for example, could not support as much farming or as many people as level areas with fertile soil. Another factor was the presence of cities. The region surrounding a large town usually had many peasant communities nearby so that the city and countryside could easily benefit from each other. In places like Scandinavia and Scotland, where there were few cities and much of the land was hard to farm, country people tended to live on isolated family farms or in small clusters of just a few farmsteads. On the other hand, in parts of eastern Europe there were villages of a thousand or more people, all of whom were needed to raise the large quantities of grain or livestock that the lords exported to the west. Elsewhere, a good-sized village might be home to between thirty and fifty families.

# TRADITIONAL VILLAGES

In fertile farming areas, such as those in southern England and most of France, many villages followed a pattern that was hundreds of years old. The villagers' homes and gardens clustered together, typically on either side of a wide dirt road. Depending on the size of the village, there could be some smaller roads branching off the main one. A river or stream usually flowed not far from the houses. The water might turn a mill wheel to power machinery that ground grain into flour. Some places had windmills instead of, or in addition to, water-powered mills.

At a little distance from the villagers' homes, the landlord (if there

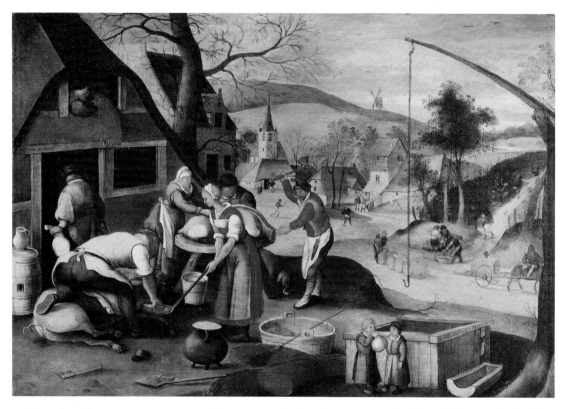

*Near the village center, peasants spend an autumn day butchering pigs so that they will have smoked and salted pork to eat during the winter. In the foreground on the right, two children are playing with an inflated pig bladder, a kind of Renaissance balloon.*

# The Village Church

Most villages had a church. It was usually built of stone and was sometimes the only stone building in the area. The inside of a country church might be decorated with wall paintings showing scenes from the Bible. There could also be a few statues of Jesus and of some of the saints. There were generally no pews—churchgoers had to stand or bring stools from home. As the sixteenth century progressed, however, some Protestant churches began to have benches for worshippers to sit on.

The church could be used for other purposes besides religious services. It provided the best indoor space for meetings of the village council or assembly. And in England, church towers were often considered the ideal place for beehives. The village cemetery was in the churchyard, which was also used as an outdoor gathering place. When traveling preachers visited, they often preached in the churchyard. Some of these preachers were carrying the new Protestant teachings to the countryside. Peasants who embraced the Reformation sometimes destroyed the religious statues and the altar in their church.

The priest or minister was generally appointed by church authorities. He might be a member of a local family, familiar to the villagers since his boyhood. But even when he was a stranger, he would generally become an active member of the community. He not only led worship services and performed baptisms, marriages, and funerals, but also helped villagers with their problems, giving advice, settling disputes, visiting the sick, and so on. Some country priests did not know how to read and write, but those who did could help villagers with letters, documents, and the like. They might even give peasant children some lessons in reading and writing. Many priests were also landowners, and many enjoyed socializing with the other villagers.

was one) often had a residence. This could be a very grand manor house, surrounded by landscaped gardens and parklands. The lord might also have demesne (dih-MANE) land, acreage that he did not rent to tenants; he hired laborers to farm it for him. In addition to fields, the demesne could include orchards, sheep pens, beehives, stables, and the like. Often the landlord's house and land were enclosed by a high fence or wall.

Three large fields surrounded the village houses. Beyond the fields were woods. The woodland nearest to the village was usually reserved for the landlord's use. In woods farther off, the villagers could gather firewood and forest plants and could let their pigs loose to eat acorns and beechnuts. (If there weren't enough acorns on the ground, swineherds used long wooden poles to knock them out of the trees.) "Waste" areas between the farmland and the woods provided peasants with straw, rushes, ferns, and similar products—useful for thatching roofs, covering dirt floors, and making bedding for farm animals. There were also meadows where hay was grown and a common pasture where villagers could let their animals graze.

## Three-Field Farming

The village's three fields were farmed according to a system known as open-field or champaign agriculture. (*Champaign* is from a French word meaning "level open country"—and champaign agriculture was still practiced in parts of France well into the nineteenth century.) Each field was divided into long one-acre or half-acre strips, which were easier to plow than square plots of land. The strips were distributed among the villagers so that every farmer had some land in each field. The strips were also scattered through each field, instead of being right next to each other. In this way everyone had some of the best land, some of the worst land, and some of middle quality. To make the division of land even fairer, many village councils redistributed the strips every year or every few years. Often the strips were assigned by lottery.

*The hay meadow was a busy place in the summertime, and many people worked together to cut and gather the hay. Breaks for food, drink, and rest were also good times to socialize.*

One field would be planted in fall, one in spring, and one left fallow for the whole year. The next year the fallow field would be planted, and one of the other fields would lie fallow. This was a common form of crop rotation. In some places, instead of having a fall planting and a spring planting, farmers seeded the fields with two different crops. For instance, wheat or rye might grow in one field, while the other had oats, barley, or peas.

Another variation, becoming more common in Italy in the 1500s, was to plant alfalfa or clover in the third field instead of letting it lie fallow. This had been a common practice in Spain for a long time. Many Italian estate owners were influenced not only by the Spanish example but also by new translations of ancient Roman books about agriculture. These writings taught landlords that alfalfa and similar plants not only provided food for livestock but also enriched the soil.

## SHEEP AND HEDGES

During the Renaissance, wool was big business. All over Europe the demand for wool was growing, and landowners in some places could make huge profits by raising sheep. This was especially true in England, which produced some of the very finest wool. By 1500, large amounts of land were being converted from raising crops to raising sheep. If a lord switched to sheep farming on his demesne, most of his laborers were put out of work. It took a fairly large number of people to work the fields, but only a few shepherds to take care of sheep. Landlords might also evict their tenants and turn the fields into sheep pastures. Many unemployed farmworkers ended up moving to London and other cities to look for work. Too often, the only way they could support themselves was by begging. The tremendous growth and impact of English sheep farming prompted one writer in 1598 to compose this bitter verse:

> Sheep have eat up our meadows and our downs,
> Our corn,* our wood, whole villages and towns.      [grain]
> Yea, they have eat up many wealthy men,
> Besides widows and orphan childeren,
> Besides our statutes and our iron laws
> Which they have swallowed down into their maws.*      [stomachs]

When fields were converted to sheep pastures, landlords usually enclosed the land with walls or hedges. The practice of enclosure also came to affect crop growing in many areas. In central England, for instance, champaign agriculture was being replaced by what was called farming "in several." Landlords, investors from the cities, and even prosperous peasants

*Sheepshearing in the early sixteenth century. This painting, by Simon Bening, comes from a splendid manuscript that was made for a noble family.*

# In a Land of Grapes and Olives

In the north Italian region of Tuscany only a few isolated areas had traditional villages with fields shared among different peasant families. Instead, by 1400 the countryside was mostly a patchwork of plots of land called *poderi*. Each *podere* was farmed by a single family, who were sharecroppers. The land was actually owned by someone else, who might live in a villa on the *podere*, or in Florence or another city.

The sharecroppers kept half of what they raised and gave the other half to the landowner. A sharecropper's home was usually in the middle of the *podere*, surrounded by fields, vineyards, olive groves, pastures, and woods. Sharecroppers on the *poderi* tended to live fairly well, though simply. The land they worked was passed down from father to son, so there was a sense of security. They usually produced very profitable products, such as olive oil and wine. This meant they could afford nutritious food, comfortable houses, and good wool and linen for their homemade clothes.

were purchasing more land. As a landowner got control of larger portions of village fields, he was often able to have the strips of farmland redistributed so that all of his land was together in a single plot. Then he enclosed his plot with hedges, and that land was no longer available for common open-field farming. In this way, all of a village's farmland could end up under the ownership and control of a relatively small number of people, with no common land left for anyone else's use. Poor peasants, who could not buy up sizable blocks of land to support themselves, struggled harder than ever to make a living.

# Three

# HOME SWEET HOME

Country homes could vary tremendously, depending not only on the wealth of the family but also on what resources were available. In places where wood was scarce, houses might be built of stone, brick, or even turf. A common construction method in much of western Europe was wattle and daub. The wattle was a wall of vertical wooden posts with flexible sticks woven between them. This was filled in and plastered on both sides with the daub, a mixture of mud and straw. (In the period shortly after the Renaissance, English settlers built wattle and daub houses in Jamestown, Virginia, where reconstructed examples can be seen today.)

In some mountainous areas, roofs were made with wooden shingles, which were weighted with stones so that they would not be blown off by high winds. Where clay was plentiful, roofs might be tiled. A great many country homes had thatched roofs. Straw thatch had many advantages.

*A peasant couple cook a meal at their fireside. This picture is part of a larger wall painting made for an Italian palace.*

First, straw was easy to come by. Second, the roof straw could provide emergency food for farm animals in hard times. Third, when it was time for a new roof, the old thatch made an excellent fertilizer when it was plowed into the fields. And although new thatch was highly flammable, a thatched roof that had been exposed to many rains and snowfalls was surprisingly fire resistant.

Peasants could not build new houses or repair old ones without permission from the lord or the village council. They had to follow local regulations about getting building materials from quarries or forests. Use of these resources was carefully controlled. In western Germany, for example, five large trees were required to build a house or barn. Ordinances might even specify how thatch should be woven at the rooftop, how wall planks should be arranged, or how the clay should be mixed for wattle and daub construction. Approval was also needed for digging wells, building walls, and the like.

## MAGNIFICENT MANORS

Wealthy landowners and lords often had large, luxurious country houses. There was no standard design, but a modest English manor house typically had a central great hall with a two-story wing on each side. In front of the house was a courtyard, entered through a gatehouse. Along the sides of this forecourt were stables, barns, and storage buildings. Behind the house, arranged around another courtyard, were buildings for baking, brewing ale, making cheese and butter, and doing laundry. The whole complex was sometimes surrounded by a moat. The house's toilets emptied into the moat, but people still fished in it and let their horses drink from it.

Inside the house, the great hall had a huge fireplace, lofty ceiling, and walls covered with tapestries and wood paneling. (These houses tended to be chilly. Tapestries, besides being decorative, helped cut down on drafts.) High up on one wall might be a minstrels' gallery, a balcony where musicians played to entertain the lord's family and their guests on special occasions. On an average day, however, the lord and his family dined privately in a parlor on the ground floor of one wing of the house. A stairway led from the parlor to a solar, a well furnished room with several windows. It could be used as a living room, a study, or a place for the women of the family to work on their sewing and embroidery. The other wing of the house had a pantry and kitchen on the ground floor and bedrooms above. There might also be a chapel where the family and servants attended worship services, especially if the manor house was a good distance from the nearest church.

*This villa, with its splendid gardens, was owned by the Medici family, who ruled Florence, Italy, during the Renaissance. It was used as a hunting lodge and country getaway.*

Even grander were some of the country villas built for nobles or wealthy merchant-bankers in Italy. Some of these villas were at the center of large farming estates, where rents from tenants and sales of farm products were landowners' main incomes. Other villas were more like "weekend getaways" for wealthy city dwellers who enjoyed having a break from their busy urban lives. The most magnificent villas were designed by noted architects, who were often influenced by ancient Greek and Roman architecture. For instance, several notable villas designed by Andrea Palladio, in the region around Venice, had entryways that looked very much like the facades of ancient temples. In other villas, Greek and Roman influence was obvious in the use of columns, rows of arches, and courtyard fountains and statues. Many Italian country homes were decorated, inside and out, with frescos illustrating family history or scenes from mythology.

## HOMES FOR THE "MIDDLING SORT"

Well-off peasants did not live in the grandeur of lords, but they were fairly comfortable. For example, Francis Drake came from a prosperous peasant family in southern England. (He later became the first Englishman to sail around the world, and a great favorite at Queen Elizabeth I's court.) The Drake farm was about a mile away from a town called Tavistock. When Drake was born in 1540, his family probably had more than a hundred acres of land. The property included a house, barns and stables, a building for brewing ale, sheep pens and pigsties, orchards, gardens, meadows, and woods, as well as fields for crop growing.

In Drake's family, the house and farm buildings were arranged along the sides of a narrow courtyard. The house, built of stone, was a longhouse, a type common in sixteenth-century England. A single fireplace and chimney divided the inside of the house into two areas. One was for farm ani-

*Two travelers are given rest and refreshment outside the home of prosperous French peasants. The "middling sort" could afford to be generous, while poor peasant families had hardly enough food, drink, and shelter for themselves.*

mals. It probably had a stone floor and a drainage channel in the center, to make it easier to clean up after the animals. Keeping them inside, especially in the winter, helped protect them from the elements and from thieves, and their body heat contributed to the house's warmth. (Unfortunately, the animals' presence also made the house a good deal smellier!)

The fireplace, the only source of heat, faced the house's other section, the main living area. The family had a fire even in warm weather, because all cooking was done at the fireplace. Next to the fireplace there was a stairway that went up into a one- or two-room loft. The loft was used for storage and for sleeping. People also slept in the main living area below, but there were no separate bedrooms. The living area was one large room, perhaps fifteen feet square, with simple furniture.

The mother of William Shakespeare, the great English writer, also came from a well-to-do farm family. When her father died, she inherited his hundred acres, his house and barn (filled with stored wheat and barley), and numerous farm animals. The house was well furnished with oak furniture, copper and brass pans, and eleven cloth wall hangings, which were painted with scenes from Bible stories and Roman mythology.

## COUNTRY COTTAGES

The majority of peasants lived in one- or two-room cottages, sometimes hardly better than huts. Many had no chimneys, only a gap in the roof to allow smoke to escape. While prosperous homes often had wood, tile, or stone floors, the houses of poorer country folk had floors of hard-packed dirt. People covered the ground with loose straw or rushes, sometimes with herbs and flowers mixed in.

Poor families had little furniture. They might not even have beds, only straw-stuffed mattresses that they laid out on the floor when it was

# A Good Night's Sleep

In 1587 William Harrison wrote a *Description of England*. In it he remarked, "There are old men yet dwelling in the village where I remain, which have noted three things to be marvellously altered in England within their sound remembrance." One of these marvelous changes was "the great amendment (although not general) of lodging"—the improvement that many (but not all) people were enjoying in their sleeping conditions:

> [F]or, said they, our fathers (yea, and we ourselves also) have lain full oft upon straw pallets, covered only with a sheet, under coverlets made of . . . [coarse material]. . . , and a good round log under our heads instead of a bolster or pillow. If it were so that our fathers or the goodman of the house had within seven years after his marriage purchased a mattress or flockbed, and thereto a sack of chaff to rest his head upon, he thought himself to be as well lodged as the lord of the town . . . so well were they contented. Pillows, said they, were thought meet only for women in childbed. As for servants, if they had any sheet above them, it was well, for seldom had they any under their bodies, to keep them from the pricking straws that ran oft through the canvas of the pallet, and razed their hardened hides.

time to go to sleep. They sat on stools, benches, or the ground. Some people had permanent tables, but others just laid a board across two supports when they needed a table. Some had to make do without even this, setting out their main meal on a single platter balanced on a stool. Plates and dishes were made out of wood for the poor, pewter for the better-off.

## THE DARK AND DIRTY SIDE OF LIFE

In manor, villa, longhouse, or cottage, there were some conditions shared by all: There was no electricity and no indoor plumbing. Without electricity, there were not many choices for lighting. During the day, light came from the fire and from a few windows, which could be shuttered at night. Well-to-do people had glass in their windows. Others had to make do with oiled paper or perhaps animal skin. In some parts of the English countryside, wicker or oak-slat lattices were set into the windows. During the night, oil lamps were available in some places. Candles, especially beeswax ones, were expensive, so only better-off people could afford to use them much. They were sometimes placed inside lanterns to protect the flame. Generally people had to make do with firelight and perhaps moonlight shining through the windows. Most of the time peasants just went to bed when it got dark.

The lack of indoor plumbing affected people in many ways. Laundry usually had to be washed in a nearby stream or river. This was a time-consuming job, so it was usually done only one or two times a month. When water was needed for cooking, drinking, cleaning, or other household uses, it had to be hauled from the river or stream or drawn from a well. Some households had their own well. In other places, everyone might have to share one or two village wells. If hot water was needed, it had to be heated in a pot or kettle over the fire.

Without indoor plumbing and hot water heaters, a bath was a major undertaking. Well-off people might own barrel-like wooden bathtubs, and

# Peasant Food

Here is a simple meal you can enjoy today that is similar to what a French peasant might have eaten during the Renaissance:

**Vegetable broth or bouillon:** Make according to the directions on the can or package. When it is heated, add some fresh or frozen peas and carrots (cut up or sliced) and let them cook for a few minutes in the liquid.

**Salad:** If you have a garden, you can pick your own lettuces and herbs. Otherwise use a bag of fresh spring or baby salad greens. If you want to, add some fresh herbs, such as thyme, savory, marjoram, tarragon, or rosemary. Use a simple dressing of oil and vinegar (the French poet Ronsard recommended walnut oil and red wine vinegar for country salads).

**Bread:** To eat like a prosperous peasant, you could buy a loaf of French bread. Whole wheat or multigrain bread, from a bakery or baked at home, would be closest to what most people ate. Or you could have unsweetened cornbread—after the Spanish brought maize from the Americas, peasants in some parts of France (and much of northern Italy) commonly ate cornmeal cakes instead of wheat bread.

**Cheese:** Chèvre (goat cheese) and Brie are types of cheese that were often eaten in the French countryside. Swiss cheese, cream cheese, and Gouda are similar to other kinds of cheese made during the Renaissance.

**Cider:** In much of France, wine was the most common drink for people of all ages and all classes. But the region of Normandy in northern France was famous for its orchards and for its delicious apple and pear ciders.

*Bon appétit!*

might use them about once a week. Most country dwellers, though, seem to have made do with a sponge bath now and then, at least in summer. During the winter in much of Europe, it was too cold to consider bathing. But people generally did wash their faces and hands regularly and rubbed their teeth clean with bits of cloth.

There were no flush toilets, of course. Manor houses often had indoor privies that emptied into a moat, ditch, or cesspit. At the average peasant's home, there was an outhouse or two in the yard behind the house. Rich and poor country dwellers alike also used chamber pots, especially at night or in bad weather. These were later emptied outdoors.

# four

# COUNTRY FOLKS

ometimes today we think of a village in "old times" as being a place where everyone was basically the same. Of course villagers had many shared concerns, and community spirit was especially strong where land was farmed in common. But there were also great differences between rich and poor in Renaissance villages. These differences could lead to resentment, jealousy, and competition. Landlords and rich peasants often took advantage of the poor, and village society was always dominated by the wealthier and more powerful members of the community.

## LANDLORDS AND THEIR AGENTS

The wealthy Italian merchants and bankers who owned rural villas usually spent most of their time in the nearby city, attending to business. Every so often they made the short trip out to the country to spend a few days at

*A northern Italian landowner fingers his money bag as he listens to the concerns of one of his tenants. The man behind the tenant is probably the lord's bailiff or steward.*

their villas. There they could take long, peaceful walks alone in their gardens, or they could entertain friends and enjoy conversation, music, banquets, and the like. They were not very concerned with farming or other country matters, although such subjects might occasionally crop up in conversation.

City-dwelling landowners and those who spent most of their time at court were rarely seen by their tenants. But peasants were very familiar with some of the landlord's employees. There was usually a steward who managed the lord's demesne. He could also be the person in charge of dealing with the tenants for the lord. On behalf of the lord, the steward might judge legal cases that arose among villagers. (Serious cases, however, generally had to be handled by royal, not local, authorities.) Sometimes the steward was the lord's rent collector, too. Otherwise another employee, often called a bailiff, handled this unpopular job.

## COUNTRY GENTLEMEN

On small or middle-sized estates, at least in some areas, the lord often took an active interest in farming his lands. This was especially true of much of the lower nobility in France during the sixteenth century. These lords felt a true attachment to their estates, which had been handed down through their families for generations. They felt responsible for taking care not only of their land but also of the people who lived on it. Such landowners knew their tenants and the other villagers personally and frequently socialized with them. They were ready with advice, medicinal herbs from their gardens, and other assistance for the peasants who depended on them.

A country gentleman of this sort led a very active life. He supervised a large number of farmworkers and handled rents and other matters with his tenants. He arranged for the sale of surplus grain and other products, and inspected the health of animals before they were sold at market. He patrolled his lands to make sure that fences and walls were in good repair, that hedges had no breaks, and that irrigation or drainage ditches were not blocked. He planned out gardens and decided what crops to plant and when to plant them. The landowner who personally ran his estate knew exactly when it was the right time to do all the necessary farm tasks, and he knew the best way to do them. If he was away at war or for some other reason, his wife often managed the estate until he returned.

Some country gentlemen even enjoyed doing farmwork themselves. Noël du Fail, a minor nobleman, was this kind of gentleman-farmer. He was also an author, and described his pleasure in working and living on the land:

> In the orchard you'll find me at work with my billhook and pruning hook, my sleeves rolled back, cutting, trimming, and pruning my young bushes according to the moon. . . . In the

*In a carefully tended orchard, between a row of trees, farmworkers cut and rake the grass for hay.*

garden, creating order according to my plan, straightening up the square of the paths, training this way and that the flowers and roots . . . and getting mad with the moles and voles which do me so much harm, and sowing various and strange seeds; mixing and blending the warm earth with the cold, watering the dry parts, forcing the late fruits, and controlling by knowing tricks, commonly ignored, the effects and results of nature. In the woods, I am deepening my ditches, aligning my walks, and meanwhile listening to a hundred bird songs and getting my workmen to recount a raft of rustic tales. By the streams, amused and solitary on the bank, I fish with a line. . . . Sometimes, too, with a leash of greyhounds and eight running dogs, I shall be out hunting foxes, roebuck, or hares, without knocking down or damaging the laborers' wheat, as do some breakers of the law and common justice.

# Shakespeare in the Country

William Shakespeare is regarded as England's greatest poet and playwright. He was born and grew up in Stratford-upon-Avon, a small market town. Sometime in the 1580s he became an actor, moved to London, and soon began to write plays. He returned to his hometown frequently and eventually became a prominent landowner there. Stratford had close relations with the surrounding countryside, and so did Shakespeare—some of his relatives were farmers and lived in villages only a few miles away. Shakespeare's personal experience and his imagination combined to help him write the following scenes of country life.

## A Harsh Season

The comedy *Love's Labour's Lost* ends with a little play in which an actor recites this poetic portrayal of winter in the country:

> *When icicles hang by the wall,*
> *   And Dick the shepherd blows his nail,*
> *And Tom bears logs into the hall,*
> *   And milk comes frozen home in pail;*
> *When blood is nipped, and ways be foul,*
> *Then nightly sings the staring owl:*
> *Tu-whit, tu-whoo!—a merry note,*
> *While greasy Joan doth keel\* the pot.*                    [skim]

When all aloud the wind doth blow,
    *And coughing drowns the parson's saw,\**           [sermon]
*And birds sit brooding in the snow,*
    *And Marian's nose looks red and raw;*
*When roasted crabs\* hiss in the bowl,*           [crab apples]
*Then nightly sings the staring owl:*
*Tu-whit, tu-whoo!—a merry note,*
*While greasy Joan doth keel the pot.*

—Act V, Sc. 2

## Popular Beliefs

*A Midsummer Night's Dream,* one of Shakespeare's most popular comedies, was influenced by folklore about fairies and other "sprites" (spirits). This conversation between a fairy and the mischievous (but sometimes helpful) spirit known as Robin Goodfellow expresses some of the beliefs held by many country people:

FAIRY:
*Either I mistake your shape and making quite*
*Or else you are that shrewd and knavish sprite*
*Called Robin Goodfellow. Are not you he*
*That frights the maidens of the villag'ry,*
*Skim milk, and sometimes labour in the quern,\**   [hand mill for grinding grain]
*And bootless\* make the breathless housewife churn,*       [uselessly]
*And sometime make the drink to bear no barm\*—*         [yeast]

*Although some experts disagree, this is probably an authentic portrait of William Shakespeare. The great playwright seems to have been equally at home in country and city.*

Mislead night wanderers, laughing at their harm?
Those that "hobgoblin" call you, and "sweet puck,"
You do their work, and they shall have good luck.
Are you not he?

ROBIN:                    Thou speak'st aright;
I am that merry wanderer of the night.
I jest to Oberon,* and make him smile                    [the king of the fairies]
When I a fat and bean-fed horse beguile,
Neighing in likeness of a filly foal;
And sometime lurk I in a gossip's* bowl                    [old woman's]
In very likeness of a roasted crab*,                    [crabapple]
And when she drinks, against her lips I bob,
And on her withered dewlap* pour the ale.                    [loose skin on the neck]
The wisest aunt telling the saddest tale
Sometime for three-foot stool mistaketh me;
Then slip I from her bum. Down topples she,
And "tailor" cries, and falls into a cough,
Then the whole choir* hold their hips, and laugh,                    [group]
And waxen* in their mirth, and sneeze, and swear                    [increase]
A merrier hour was never wasted there.

—Act II, Sc. 1

# PEASANTS RICH AND POOR

It took twenty to forty acres for a peasant to produce enough food to feed a family and pay rents, taxes, and tithes. At the higher end of this range, peasants might even have a little surplus that they could sell at a market. If they earned enough money through such sales, they could rent or purchase more land and hire laborers to help them work it. The more land peasants had, the more surplus they could produce—this was nearly the only way for a peasant family to prosper. Some families did become quite well off by building up their land holdings. Such success was easiest to achieve when peasants could own their own land instead of having to pay rents, which were always rising. In most areas the number of families farming a hundred or more acres was fairly low—perhaps only two or three out of a village of some sixty households.

Families with only twenty or so acres just managed to get by, so long as crops were good. A bad harvest, though, could quickly plunge them into poverty. It was even worse for those with less land. They simply could not raise enough to support themselves. These peasants had to work as laborers for others or find other ways to supplement their incomes. They had little hope of improving their situation. They could not afford to eat any of their pigs, chickens, or eggs, or any of the good fruit that grew on the trees in their gardens. All such products had to be sold just so that these families could pay their rents.

Some of the poorest peasants had only a cottage and garden. As William Harrison wrote in his *Description of England* (1587), "a poor man . . . thinketh himself very friendly dealt withal if he may have an acre of ground assigned unto him whereon to keep a cow, or wherein to set cabbages, radishes, parsnips, carrots, melons, pompions [pumpkins] or suchlike stuff, by which he and his poor household liveth as by their principal food, sith [since] they can do no better." Poor peasants often went to work for rich ones and sometimes borrowed money from them so that they could buy food.

No matter how hard they worked, some peasants still could not make ends meet. They might end up wandering from village to village, sur-

*Tax collectors, such as these two men, were almost universally disliked. Many peasants barely managed to produce enough to feed themselves and pay their rents and taxes.*

viving by doing odd jobs, begging, scavenging, stealing, or a combination of these. If they went to a city, they might be lucky enough to find work or to get other help from one of the charitable organizations that many urban communities supported. Unfortunately, poverty, hunger, and homelessness were problems as difficult to solve in the Renaissance as they are now.

# five

# WORK, WORK, WORK

Renaissance peasants worked from sunup till sundown, taking advantage of every hour of daylight. The whole family worked, too, except for very young children. Everyone's labor was absolutely necessary for the family to be able to survive. In general, men did the work out in the fields and women worked in and around the house and garden. But women could and did work in the fields, especially at haymaking and harvest time, when every hand was needed.

## THE YEAR'S PATTERN

Much farmwork was determined by the time of year and the weather, so the work varied depending on the climate and other conditions in different regions of Europe. For example, many French and Italian peasants tended vineyards, and their activities included the various stages of growing grapes

*Harvesting grapes in Italy. The woman on the left has tucked up her long skirts so that she can easily climb the ladder to reach grapes on a vine that has been trained to grow up a tree. Down the hill a large vineyard stretches into the distance.*

and making wine. English peasants might be involved in producing cider, since apple trees were plentiful in much of England. Southern Europeans were often able to plant and harvest many weeks earlier than northern Europeans because of the warmer climate. But despite the differences, peasants everywhere followed similar yearly patterns.

Every month had its own labors. January was generally the time for pruning vines and fruit trees, making sure all the farm tools were in good repair, and starting to turn the soil in the garden and in the field that would be planted in spring. Some of these labors continued into February, which was also the month for sorting seeds and cleaning out beehives and henhouses. Sheep began to give birth to lambs in February, so shepherds became very busy tending their flocks, and in some places farmwives milked the ewes and made sheep-milk cheese.

The main task in March was to get the fields and gardens planted. Women and children also gathered fresh spring greens, such as violet and dandelion leaves, to make nutritious salads. In April, fields and gardens needed to be weeded, and fruit trees could be planted. May was the month for sheepshearing, making cheese and butter, picking strawberries, watering young trees, and more weeding. It parts of France and Italy, peasants collected silkworm cocoons from mulberry trees in May.

Haymaking was June's big job. The hay could only be cut on sunny days (giving us the proverb "Make hay while the sun shines"), so that it could be spread out on the meadows to dry. Then it was gathered into haystacks or loaded into carts to be taken to the barns for storage. Other June tasks were cleaning the threshing floor (where harvested grain would be separated from stalks and seed coverings), harvesting barley, and picking rose petals and herbs to make rosewater, medicines, and other products.

In July peasants could begin to harvest the wheat that had been sown the previous fall. They also removed bad fruit from trees so that the remaining fruit would ripen better, and they fertilized grapevines and fruit trees with manure. Harvesting continued in August—along with the grain, melons and cucumbers were now ripe. In France peasants also harvested flax (for making linen) and hemp (for making rope), and in the vineyards they cut away leaves that shaded the ripening grapes from the sun.

September was the month to sow the fall planting of wheat, rye, or other grains. Threshing, begun in July or August, continued. Apples, grapes, and walnuts were ready to be picked. Grain, vegetable, and fruit seeds were saved for the next spring planting, and straw was gathered for thatching. Swineherds drove pigs into the woods to eat acorns, while other people went to the woods to start gathering extra firewood for the coming winter. Many farm animals were now taken to the butcher or sold at the market.

*Harvesting grain was August's big job in much of Europe. In this painting by Simon Bening, a woman ties up sheaves of harvested wheat as two men with sickles continue to cut more grain. In the background a heavily laden cart carries bound sheaves away to a barn.*

In October, people harvested honey and beeswax from the beehives and gathered flexible twigs, vines, and other materials for making baskets. For grape-growing areas, this was also the month for wine making. November was the time to carry out final preparations for winter. In Italy and France, it was also the month for pressing olives to make olive oil. Then, in December, farm families settled down to making baskets and other utensils, making or mending tools, spinning and weaving, and other indoor tasks.

## MORE WAYS TO MAKE A LIVING

It was very common for villagers to do other work along with, or even instead of, farmwork. A great many peasants, especially women, did spinning and weaving in their homes for cloth manufacturers in the towns. English peasant women often brewed and sold ale, and French and Italian peasants might sell wine. Women sometimes baked extra bread to sell to their neighbors, too. Men made extra money by hauling goods in their carts.

Peasant women were often the ones who took eggs, cheeses, and other produce to sell at town markets. Some prosperous peasants were able to engage in selling on a larger scale. They became rural merchants, dealing in grain, wool, and perhaps wine, which they sold in nearby villages and towns. Well-to-do peasants could also earn money by loaning small sums—to be repaid with interest—to their less fortunate neighbors. Some peasants rented their extra horses or oxen to others.

Most villages had at least a few craftspeople or tradespeople—a blacksmith, a carpenter, a shoemaker, a dressmaker, a miller, for example. Sometimes there was also a notary, a man who could read and write documents and draw up contracts for the villagers. In areas where there was a lot of clay, some villagers manufactured tiles and bricks.

Another important job carried on in the countryside was mining. For instance, there were coal mines in northern England and tin mines in southwestern England. In Germany and Hungary there were rich veins of

*In a Dutch market around 1560, two peasants from the countryside prepare to sell some of their chickens and eggs. The woman also has a couple loaves of bread, and the man has a number of small birds, which he probably snared in the hedges or woods near his farm.*

gold, silver, copper, iron, and lead. However, miners were often poorly paid, and their working conditions were uncomfortable and dangerous. In compensation, miners might be exempt from serving in the military or paying certain taxes. All the same, peasant men were less and less willing to work as miners. In some areas, working in the mines became a punishment for criminals.

Peasants who lived near a river or the ocean often earned part of their livelihood from fishing. In the Basque country of southwestern France and northwestern Spain, for example, there was a tradition of long-distance

# Sailors and Soldiers

The Renaissance's voyages of exploration led to increasing seaborne trade in many nations and to the growth of naval forces to protect overseas shipping. Boys and men in coastal areas might have the opportunity to go to sea instead of farming. As a boy, Francis Drake, for example, was sent from his family's farm to be educated in the home of his seafaring relative John Hawkins. By the time he was in his teens, Drake was sailing with Hawkins and his sons to ports in France, Spain, and the Netherlands. The Hawkins family were fairly successful merchants, but they also engaged in piracy from time to time. This was not an unusual career path for sixteenth-century men who went to sea.

Some male peasants became soldiers. Renaissance rulers were constantly increasing the size of their armies. Before 1500 a typical army was made up of between 10,000 and 30,000 men; in 1570 the number was as high as 85,000. Commanders were generally nobles or well-born gentlemen, but the common soldiers were drawn from among poor peasants and townsmen. Some were recruited by force, or were obligated to provide military service to their lord. Other men enlisted voluntarily, since they might not have any other way to make a living—or they might simply crave adventure. Many of these became mercenaries, soldiers for hire, who would fight in any army that paid them decently.

fishing and whaling expeditions. In fact, the Basques were probably fishing for cod off the coast of Canada at least a hundred years before Columbus landed in the Caribbean. But since the Basques could sell salted cod for high prices and they did not want competition, they never told anyone else about the New World and its fertile fishing grounds.

# Six

# FAMILY LIFE

A typical peasant household included parents, children, and sometimes a few other relatives, such as a widowed parent or unmarried sibling of the husband or wife. Mothers gave birth to an average of five or six children, but often only two or three lived through childhood. Prosperous peasants generally had a few servants, who might also live with the family. Most households had a cat, to keep down rodents, and perhaps a dog or two, to guard the home and livestock. These cats and dogs may often have been treated with affection, but most people probably thought of them more as working farm animals than as pets.

## BIRTH AND BABIES

All babies were born at home. Birth was a frightening and dangerous experience because there were not many medical techniques to help out if some-

*This painting of shepherds adoring the newborn Jesus, as described in the Bible, shows how Renaissance babies were often tightly swaddled to keep them feeling warm and secure. Many people also thought that swaddling was necessary to make sure a baby's arms and legs would grow properly.*

thing went wrong. In fact, few villages had doctors at all. Women in child-birth often had little more than prayers and traditional customs to rely on for help. For example, in the Italian countryside it was common for a husband (who was usually not allowed to be present) to give his wife his cap to wear for good luck during labor.

Fortunately, many peasants had a good knowledge of herbal medicine, and almost every village had at least one experienced midwife. Midwives were usually older women who not only helped deliver babies but also treated women's health problems. Still, no one in Renaissance Europe knew about germs, so no measures were taken to prevent infection. Even with the help of a skilled midwife, many mothers and babies died during or soon after childbirth.

Unlike many upper-class women, peasant mothers nursed their own children, usually for a year or two. (Sometimes, especially if her own baby died, a peasant woman could earn extra money by nursing and taking care of a child from a noble or wealthy city family.) If a mother died, or could not nurse her baby for some other reason, the child was given goat's or cow's milk from a baby bottle made out of a cow's horn.

Mothers had to go back to work within a few days of giving birth. Often they would carry the baby along with them in a cloth sling or similar carrier. Sometimes babies and toddlers were left in the care of an elderly relative or neighbor, or an older sister might be responsible for looking after younger siblings. Sadly, there were times when peasant parents, with heavy work to do in the fields, had to leave babies or young children alone in the cottage. The children had to wait until the end of the long workday to be fed and tended, and in the meantime they risked injury and even death from fires or accidents.

## GROWING UP

Almost as soon as children could walk, they started helping with their parents' work. They stood guard in gardens, fields, and orchards, chasing off birds that might eat seeds or crops. They gathered nuts, berries, and herbs in the woods and meadows. Even fairly young children could pull weeds in gardens and scatter feed for the family's chickens. Older children could take more responsibility for tending sheep, cows, geese, and other farm animals. At home they could fetch water from the well, and in the fields they could sow seeds and bind up sheaves of harvested grain.

In some villages, children might have the opportunity to attend school for a couple of years. They would learn basic reading, writing, and

*Two schoolteachers work with students individually while the other pupils study their lessons. Schools like this one often taught poor children for free but expected fees for children from well-to-do families.*

arithmetic. A few boys, usually from prosperous families, might continue their schooling and eventually even attend a university. Sometimes a village child became an apprentice to a craftsperson and learned a skilled trade.

The majority of peasant children were educated mostly by observing and assisting their parents. Fathers showed their sons how to make and repair tools. Mothers showed their daughters how to spin, cook, and keep house. Children learned to plant and harvest, to prune trees and vines, to handle livestock, and to master countless other skills by working alongside their parents.

During the teenage years, children usually had the same workload as adults. They didn't always stay at home to work, though. In some areas it was customary for teenage boys to leave the village and go up into the mountains to tend flocks of sheep for the summer. In other places, young adult males commonly joined the crews of fishing fleets. Numerous teenagers—especially girls, and especially from poor families—went to work as servants or hired laborers for several years. For many girls, this was the only way that they could save up a dowry, the money they would need to be able to get married.

# A Little Goatherd

Thomas Platter, who eventually became a respected printer and educator, was born into a poor peasant family in 1499. They lived high in the Swiss Alps, where weather conditions and the mountainous terrain made life especially hard. When Thomas was six years old, he went to work as a goatherd. He recalled the experience when he wrote his autobiography toward the end of his life:

> *I was so small, that when I opened the stable door and did not jump aside quickly, the goats knocked me down. I once drove my goats up to a ledge, which was one step wide, with nothing but rock below it for over a thousand fathoms. From the ledge, they climbed a rock face covered in tufts of grass. But when I had gone up the grass a small step, I could go no further, and I dared not jump back to the narrow ledge in case I jumped too far and fell over the terrible precipice. I stayed there for a good while, holding on to tufts of grass with both hands, and supported by my big toe on another tuft. I feared that the great vultures who flew below me would carry me away. . . .*

Fortunately, a friend saw Thomas's predicament and came to his rescue. After three more years of difficult and frightening experiences, Thomas's aunts, who raised him, decided he was not going to be a success as a goatherd. They arranged for him to go to school instead.

# GETTING MARRIED

Most peasants married when they were in their twenties. Occasionally they were much younger. We know of one case in southern France in which the bride may have been only ten, and the groom thirteen or fourteen. This was very unusual and probably happened because both came from very prosperous families, which were eager to be connected by marriage. Such a connection could increase the wealth and importance of both families.

Marriages were normally arranged by the families of the couple. In some places, such as parts of Italy, midwives assisted in this process by acting as matchmakers. Sometimes the groom-to-be might ask his parents to arrange for him to marry a certain girl. Usually both families were from

*Dutch peasants celebrate a wedding with a lively outdoor feast accompanied by bagpipe music. The bride is the third woman from the right; the groom is probably the man with the fur-trimmed collar.*

the same village or neighboring villages, so the couple probably knew each other at least a little before they became betrothed, or engaged.

An important part of almost every betrothal was the negotiating and signing of the marriage contract. The contract laid out the terms of the bride's dowry, which might be paid all at once or over a period of several years. A typical dowry for a girl from a well-off peasant family was a cash payment and household goods such as pillows, sheets, a bed, and a storage chest. The bride's family might also include a field or vineyard in the dowry and would probably give the young woman a trousseau of two or three dresses in different colors. The groom's family's part of the contract was mainly to promise how the bride would be provided for if her husband died.

In earlier centuries, peasant weddings had often been very informal. But after the Reformation began, both Catholic and Protestant churches came to insist that betrothals be publicly announced and that couples have formal wedding ceremonies in church. After the ceremony, it was common for a procession of villagers to accompany the bride and groom to their home, where the wedding was celebrated with a banquet.

## For Better or Worse

The Renaissance concept of marriage did not have much to do with love. Ideally, the husband and wife should be good companions, friendly and respectful to each other, and partners in caring for their family and property. If the couple were in love, or grew to love each other—and many did—that was a bonus.

Still, most people strongly believed that the husband was the head of the family, superior to his wife in every respect. This idea was expressed everywhere from sermons to jokes. If a wife acted superior to her husband, or if their marriage differed from village expectations in other ways, the young men of the village might stage a charivari at their house. This

# An Ideal
# Country Couple

This song, written by Thomas Campion for a courtly audience, contrasts a wholesome peasant life with the artificialness of life at court. Such idealizations of country living were common in ancient Greek and Roman poetry, and many Renaissance writers carried on this literary tradition.

## Jack and Joan

*Jack and Joan, they think no ill,*
*But loving live, and merry still;*
*Do their weekdays' work, and pray*
*Devotely on the holy day;*
*Skip and trip it on the green,*
*And help to choose the summer queen;*
*Lash out, at a country feast,*
*Their silver penny with the best.*

Well can they judge of nappy ale,
And tell at large a winter tale;
Climb up to the apple loft,
And turn the crabs* till they be soft.                    [crabapples]
Tib is all the father's joy,
And little Tom the mother's boy.
All their pleasure is content;
And care, to pay their yearly rent.


Joan can call by name her cows,
And deck her windows with green boughs;
She can wreathes and tuttyes* make,                    [bouquets]
And trim with plums a bridal cake.
Jack knows what brings gain or loss,
And his long flail can stoutly toss;
Make the hedge, which others break,
And ever thinks what he doth speak.


Now, you courtly dames and knights,
That study only strange delights,
Though you scorn the homespun gray,
And revel in your rich array;
Though your tongues dissemble deep,
And can your heads from danger keep;
Yet, for all your pomp and train,
Securer lives the silly* swain.*            [innocent]    [country fellow]

custom differed from place to place, but typically the young men blackened their faces, dressed up in women's clothes, sang mocking songs, and banged pots and pans outside the windows. The charivari taunted the couple, called attention to their "abnormal" marriage, and sometimes perhaps embarrassed them into behaving more traditionally.

Husbands were legally entitled to discipline their wives by hitting and even beating them. Communities tended to disapprove of men who beat their wives too often or too severely, and occasionally an abusive husband was taken to court. But an abused wife could not get a divorce— divorce was hardly ever allowed in Europe at this time. If a peasant marriage did not work out, sometimes one of the spouses (usually the husband) would desert the other. Usually, though, people just had to make the best of a bad situation.

# Seven

# REST AND RECREATION

Although people in the countryside worked long and hard, they still found time for enjoyment. They might pause in their plowing to listen to the birds singing, or gossip with friends while doing the laundry. Almost everywhere in Europe, peasants took Sunday as a day of rest. In some places they were required by law to attend church, but otherwise they were free to do as they wished with their time. Outdoor dances were often held on summer Sundays. There were also holidays when peasants could take a break from work and enjoy special festivities. Market days and fairs gave further opportunities to experience a change from the daily routine of work.

## EVERYDAY PLEASURES

Even workdays could have room for some recreation. At times when many villagers were laboring together, such as haymaking, jokes and songs made

*A group of harvesters take a rest from their work to share a meal and socialize.*

the work more pleasant. On the way home from the fields at the end of the day, friends might socialize in the village tavern. Often this was simply the home of someone who had recently brewed a batch of ale, but some villages had regular taverns or inns. Games and sports were popular with both children and adults. Peasants played checkers, chess, and dice, as well as games like blindman's buff. Wrestling, archery, and swimming were some of the favorite sports.

# Barley Break, a Renaissance Game

Barley Break was an outdoor game enjoyed by both children and adults in Renaissance England. Like most games of the time, there were many variations. This one is meant to be played by six people.

The six players are broken up into three sets of partners. Players One and Two are stationed at one end of the field or playing area, with Three and Four at the other end. Players Five and Six stand in the middle. Each pair holds hands until One and Two shout "Barley!" and Three and Four yell back, "Break!" Then One and Three run to meet each other, as do Two and Four. Five and Six try to catch at least one of the runners. If someone is caught before meeting his or her new partner, the pair will go into the middle on the next round. For example, if Two, who is running to meet Four, gets caught, then Two and Four go to the middle, while One and Three go to one end and Five and Six go to the other. But if both pairs meet up without anyone being caught, Five and Six will stay in the middle for the next round.

Like many Renaissance games, Barley Break did not have winners and losers, and there was no definite end point to the game. People simply played it for fun, and stopped when they ran out of energy!

On long winter evenings, country dwellers often enjoyed gathering at the fireside of a friend or neighbor. As the women worked on their sewing and spinning and the men repaired tools and the like, they entertained themselves with conversation and stories. The French gentleman-farmer Noël du Fail described a storyteller at such an evening gathering in the 1500s:

> And when they were all occupied with their different work, good Robin, having asked for silence, began the story of the stork, in the days when animals could talk, or how the fox stole the fish; how he got the wolf beaten by the washerwoman when he was teaching him to fish; how the dog and the cat went [on] a long journey; about the lion, king of beasts, who made the donkey his lieutenant, and wished to be king of all; about the crow who lost his cheese by singing; . . . about the fairies, and how he often spoke familiarly with them, even in the evening going down the hollow road; and that he saw them dancing a round [a circle dance], near the fountain of Cormier, to the sound of a fine musical instrument covered in red leather. . . . He said, continuing, that they came to see him, adding that they were tremendous gossips, and he would gladly have told them to shut up if he had dared. And if someone by chance fell asleep when he was telling these tall stories, . . . Master Robin took a burning hemp-stalk at one end and blew through the other end into the nose of the sleeper, making a sign with his hand not to waken him. Then he said: "God bless us! I had so much trouble learning them and here I am breaking my head setting it to work thinking, and now they don't even deign to listen to me!" And if they didn't laugh at this, the brave fellow broke wind three times, which amused them all, and then all laughed fit to bust.

# CELEBRATING THE SEASONS

In Catholic areas there were many holy days honoring various saints or events in the life of Jesus. Protestants had fewer holy days, and some of the strictest Protestants even worked on Christmas. Most country dwellers, however, greatly enjoyed the festivities of Christmastime. There was feasting, drinking of toasts, game playing, music, dancing, and singing. Some of the Christmas carols still sung today, such as "God Rest Ye Merry, Gentlemen," date back to the Renaissance. The celebrations went on for twelve full days, finishing with Twelfth Night on January 6. One of the traditions for this day was that masters and servants switched places. Another custom was to bake a cake with one bean in it. When the cake was served, whoever received the piece with the bean was the King of the Bean. He then ruled over the drinking, dancing, and other merrymaking for the rest of the feast. Sometimes the cake also contained a single pea. If a woman got it, she was Queen for the remainder of the celebration and ruled the festivities alongside the King of the Bean.

One of the best-loved country festivals in many areas was May Day (May 1), often regarded as the beginning of summer. Villagers would rise very early in the morning and wash their faces with the morning dew. Then, with music and singing, they went out to the meadows and woods to pick flowers and leafy branches; best of all were branches of the white-flowering hawthorn tree, known as Maythorn. The greenery and flowers were taken back to the village to decorate windows and doorposts and to be woven into wreaths and garlands for people to wear. An even greater prize brought from the woods was the Maypole, as an English writer described in the 1580s:

> *They have twenty or forty yoke of oxen, every oxe having a sweet nosegay of flowers placed on the tip of his horns, and these oxen draw home this Maypole . . . which is covered all over with flowers*

# An Evening's Entertainment

Noël du Fail wrote a book called *Propos rustiques* ("Rustic Observations") in 1547. In it he lovingly recorded the life of the French countryside of his time. Here he describes a festive village gathering:

> *On feast days our fathers would sooner have died than not gathered all their fold at the house of some villager, for rest and recreation after the week's work. After a drink, they began to chatter freely about the state of the crops and to listen to each other's tales. Father Jean, the late priest of our parish, was at the head of the table, to give honor where honor is due, a trifle pompous, . . . giving some good teaching . . . or conferring with the oldest of the married women, seated near him with her hood thrown back: and gladly they spoke about some herbs for fevers, colic or the grippe. . . .*
>
> *Then someone of the village would produce a rebeck [a musical instrument a bit like a violin] . . . from under his coat, or a flute, on which he played with great skill, and so seduced were they by the gentle sound of his instrument, with a hautboy [an old type of oboe] which was there to support him, that they were constrained forthwith, putting off their coats and smocks, to begin a dance. The old, to give example to the young, and to show they were not bored, had the first try, making two or three turns of the dance without kicking up their feet much or*

*Country people enjoyed lively dances, as this painting, by Pieter Brueghel the Elder, shows.*

*leaping about. . . . The young people then did their bit . . . and there was not a man there that did not dance with all the girls, except Father Jean, who had to be pressed a little, saying, "Sir, wouldn't you care to dance?" And then, having played at refusing a little, he went to it and outdid them all . . . and this venerable priest said: "Tut; tut; we never felt younger, we should take things as they come, and bad luck to anyone who halts."*

*and herbs, bound round about with strings, from the top to the bottom, and sometime painted with variable colours, with two or three hundred men, women and children following it with great devotion. And thus being reared up with handkerchiefs and flags hovering on the top, they strew the ground [with flowers] round about, bind green boughs about it, set up summer halls, bowers and arbors hard by it. And then fall they to dance about it. . . .*

Villagers often elected a King and Queen of the May to lead the dancing and direct various sports and competitions, such as races and mock swordfights. There might be entertainment by groups of singers and dancers, who went from house to house and even visited neighboring villages. Plays about Robin Hood were a May Day tradition in England.

*Morris dancers performing for the local people as well as for a group of nobles out for a country stroll. The hobbyhorse dances behind "Maid Marian," while the fool collects donations from the audience.*

Another popular English custom was morris dancing, performed by groups of men accompanied by the music of pipes and drums. The morrismen wore twenty to forty bells tied around each leg and danced in a lively style, with hops and jumps, waving handkerchiefs in their hands. They were usually led by a fool and accompanied by "Maid Marian" (a man dressed in women's clothes) and a "hobbyhorse" (a man costumed as a horse). While the morrismen danced, the fool flirted outrageously with Maid Marian. The hobbyhorse rushed in and out of the audience, teasing the members, who sometimes joined in the dancing.

Another great festival was Harvest Home, celebrating the completion of the grain harvest, usually in August. The harvesters decorated the final cartload of grain with flowers and wove a figure, often called a corn dolly, out of the last-cut stalks of grain. Then the harvest leader, crowned with a flower garland, led the cart to the barn. Men, women, and children rode on the cart or ran alongside it, singing, shouting, and passing the corn dolly from person to person. After the grain was unloaded, it was time for a feast, featuring cakes made from fresh-ground wheat and cups of frumenty, a drink made of boiled milk mixed with wheat and spices. It wasn't long before pipes, drums, and other instruments were brought out and dancing began. As one writer commented, "Oh, 'tis the merry time, wherein honest neighbours make good cheer, and God is glorified in his blessings on the earth."

# Eight

# HARD TIMES

For a great many peasants, life could be an almost continual struggle. But there were things that made hard times even harder, such as disease. During the Renaissance there were repeated epidemics of plague and smallpox. Poor sanitation led to frequent outbreaks of cholera and typhus. Since antibiotics and many other medicines were unknown, disease killed many people. Some illnesses were caused by malnutrition, for far too many peasants did not have enough protein, vitamin C, or other nutrients in their diets.

War was waged repeatedly in Renaissance Europe. Armies often devastated the countryside, raiding farms for supplies, trampling crops, burning barns, and attacking villagers. When war threatened, many peasants fled and took refuge inside the walls of nearby cities. Warfare drove some peasants away permanently, leaving fields abandoned for years, until the landlord could find new tenants. Meanwhile the fields became over-

*Poverty personified as a ragged beggar, a familiar figure to Renaissance people.*

grown with weeds and shrubs, making it hard work to clear them again for planting. It could take the countryside a very long time to recover from the ravages of war.

## PEASANT PROTESTS

When the land was at peace, harvests plentiful, and rents and taxes reasonable, peasants generally accepted the hardships of their lives. But there were many times when peasant communities were pushed to the limits of their endurance. As a result, hundreds of peasant uprisings occurred during the Renaissance. They happened all over Europe—from Spain to Hungary, from Sweden to Italy. The uprisings ranged from small protests to local riots to the formation of peasant armies.

Revolts were usually sparked because landlords, nobles, or government officials moved to reduce peasants' traditional rights and privileges. Landlords and rulers in parts of Germany, for example, were trying to take away peasants' free status and make them serfs. All over Europe, lords were claiming sole use of more forests, meadows, and waterways—and the fish, game, and other resources found in them. These claims deprived country people of much of the means of survival that they had counted on for generations. Another point of protest was the passage of new laws or judgments that differed from long-standing legal customs. Peasants were also pushed toward rebellion when landlords or rulers demanded rents, labor services, or taxes that seemed unfair or higher than they ought to be. In some areas attacks against churches and monasteries occurred because peasants resented having to pay tithes. Only once in a while did peasant uprisings have any political goals, such as gaining the right for peasants to be represented in government assemblies.

The largest rebellion, which came to be known as the German Peasants' War, took place in the 1520s. One of its inspirations was Martin Luther's message that all souls were equal before God. The peasants interpreted this to mean

*Peasants who were disabled by farm accidents or war injuries generally had no way to support themselves except by begging.*

that all people were equal on earth, too. But this was not what Martin Luther meant or believed, and he sided with the German rulers against the peasants.

By the time the Peasants' War was over, the movement had spread throughout Germany and into Switzerland, Austria, and France. It may have involved as many as 300,000 people. In addition to peasants, many craftspeople, poor city dwellers, minor nobles, and others took part. The rebels were never united under a common leadership, though. The Peasants' War was, in fact, a series of scattered uprisings rather than a single coordinated campaign.

# What Rebels Wanted

In William Shakespeare's play *Henry VI, Part 2*, a former sheepshearer and beggar named Jack Cade leads a band of peasants and craftsmen in rebellion against the "scholars, lawyers, courtiers, and gentlemen" that seem to run the kingdom. Cade promises his followers:

> *Be brave, then, for your captain is brave and vows reformation. There shall be in England seven half-penny loaves [of bread] sold for a penny, and the three-hooped pot shall have ten hoops, and I will make it a felony to drink small [weak] beer. All the realm shall be in common [common land], and in Cheapside [a business center in London] shall my palfrey [horse] go to grass. And when I am king, as king I will be . . . there shall be no money. All shall eat and drink on my score, and I will apparel them all in one livery [uniform] that they may agree like brothers, and worship [honor] me their lord.*

—Act IV, Sc. 2

Shakespeare's tragedy *Coriolanus* opens with a protest that has more serious and realistic goals than Jack Cade's. Although *Coriolanus* is set in ancient Rome, the protesters' concerns are true to what the common people of the Renaissance often felt. As the leader of the uprising explains, the poor cannot afford to buy bread, while the rich have storehouses full of grain:

> *We are accounted poor citizens, the patricians [nobles] good. What authority [those in authority] surfeits on [overindulges in] would relieve us. If they would yield us but the superfluity [extra] while it were wholesome we might guess [think] they relieved us humanely, but they think we are too dear [too expensive to take care of]. The leanness that afflicts us, the object of our*

*A rich man ignores the pleas of a beggar in this illustration from an English book published in the 1560s.*

*misery, is as an inventory to particularize their abundance; our sufferance is a gain to them. Let us revenge this with our pikes [pitchforks] ere [before] we become rakes [as thin as rakes]; for the gods know I speak this in hunger for bread, not in thirst for revenge. . . . [The nobles] ne'er cared for us yet: suffer us to famish, and their storehouses crammed with grain; make edicts for usury [moneylending at high interest] to support usurers; repeal daily any wholesome act established against the rich; and provide more piercing statutes daily to chain up and restrain the poor. If the wars eat us not up, they will; and there's all the love they bear us.*

*—Act I, Sc. 1*

The movement began peacefully in 1524 with large assemblies of peasants discussing their grievances and staging what we would call protest marches. Pamphlets were even printed and distributed in support of the peasants. But before long, rebel bands were raiding monastery storehouses,

*A peasant, armed only with a shovel, makes a desperate attempt to protect his family and farm from an invading army.*

pulling down nobles' castles and fortresses, and occupying towns. While some of these actions were orderly and highly organized, others were carried out by unruly mobs. One group of rebels even executed some captured nobles. In spite of this episode, however, it was fairly rare for the rebels to commit violence against people.

Unfortunately, government authorities had no hesitation about using violence. They sent armies of mercenary soldiers to crush the uprisings. In May of 1525, 18,000 rebels were killed in a single encounter—it could not really be called a battle, since the peasants and their allies could offer no real resistance to the professional soldiers. By the time the movement was completely dead, in the summer of 1526, as many as 100,000 people had lost their lives.

The rebels had succeeded in at least one point, however: German peasants remained free from serfdom. There were still few in Europe who believed that every person was "created equal," with "unalienable rights" to "life, liberty and the pursuit of happiness." But in just a few centuries, that idea would be embraced by a new nation in the New World. The peasants' struggles for their rights and freedom helped pave the way.

# GLOSSARY

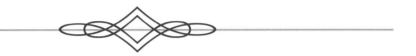

**apprentice** a young person being trained in a craft or trade by assisting and working for a master in that craft or trade

**ballad** a long, rhyming poem or song that tells a story

**bower** a shelter made from tree branches, often decorated with flowers

**broadside** a single sheet of paper, usually of a large size and sometimes folded, printed on one or both sides. Ballads were often published as broadsides.

**Catholic** refers to the branch of Christianity under the authority of the pope

**convent** common term for a women's monastery

**dowry** money, property, and goods supplied by a bride's family for her to bring into her marriage

**fallow** describes land in which no seeds are planted so that it can "rest" and regain its fertility

**fool** a clownlike character popular in Renaissance plays and celebrations

**fresco** a wall painting made on fresh plaster

**manuscript** a book that is written out, illustrated, and bound by hand

**mercenary** a soldier who fights only for money, as opposed to fighting out of loyalty to a country or cause

**monastery** a religious institution where men or women lived apart from the world, devoting themselves to prayer and study

**notary** a person who wrote out legal or official documents for individuals. Like a modern notary public, a Renaissance notary could also certify documents to make them official.

*podere* in northern Italy, a plot of land owned by a landlord and worked by a sharecropper

**Protestant** refers to Christians who reject the authority of the pope and many practices and beliefs of the Catholic Church

**Reformation** the movement begun in 1517 by Martin Luther to reform the Church. Eventually the Reformation resulted in the founding of many different kinds of Christian groups, such as Lutherans, Anglicans (Episcopalians), Calvinists (Presbyterians), and Baptists.

**saint** a person recognized by the Catholic Church as being especially holy and able to perform miracles both during life and after death

**serf** an unfree peasant, not allowed to leave the landlord's estate or to marry someone from off the estate, and owing various fees and a set amount of work to the landlord

**tithe** a kind of tax collected by the church; it was supposed to be one-tenth of a household's income

# FOR FURTHER READING

Ashby, Ruth. *Elizabethan England*. New York: Benchmark Books, 1999.

Caselli, Giovanni. *The Renaissance and the New World*. New York: Peter Bedrick, 1985.

Howarth, Sarah. *Renaissance People*. Brookfield, CT: Millbrook Press, 1992.

Howarth, Sarah. *Renaissance Places*. Brookfield, CT: Millbrook Press, 1992.

Merlo, Claudio. *Three Masters of the Renaissance: Leonardo, Michelangelo, Raphael*. Translated by Marion Lignana Rosenberg. Hauppauge, NY: Barron's Educational Series, 1999.

Mühlberger, Richard. *What Makes a Bruegel a Bruegel?* New York: The Metropolitan Museum of Art/Viking, 1993.

Netzley, Patricia D. *Life During the Renaissance*. San Diego: Lucent Books, 1998.

# ON-LINE INFORMATION*

Annenberg/CPB. *Renaissance*.
   http://www.learner.org/exhibits/renaissance
*The Artchive: Renaissance Art*.
   http://artchive.com/artchive/renaissance.html
*European Renaissance and Reformation Chronology*.
   http://www.keha.dk/Seminarium%20Homepage/English/Engelsk%20Renaisssance/
   renaissance.htm
Jokinen, Anniina. *16th Century Renaissance English Literature (1485–1603)*.
   http://www.luminarium.org/renlit
*A Journey through the Renaissance*.
   http://library.thinkquest.org/C00555356/journey.htm
Kren, Emil, and Daniel Marx. *Web Gallery of Art: Guided Tours*.
   http://gallery.euroweb.hu/tours/index.html
*Renaissance*.
   http://renaissance.dm.net
Secara, Maggie. *Life in Elizabethan England: A Compendium of Common
   Knowledge*.
   http://renaissance.dm.net/compendium/home.html
*The Shakespeare Resource Center*.
   http://www.bardweb.net
*Sites on Shakespeare and the Renaissance*.
   http://web.uvic.ca/shakespeare/Annex/ShakSites1.html

*Websites change from time to time. For additional on-line information, check with the media specialist at
your local library.

# BIBLIOGRAPHY

Barber, C. L. *Shakespeare's Festive Comedy: A Study of Dramatic Form and Its Relation to Social Custom.* Princeton, NJ: Princeton University Press, 1959.

Bell, Rudolph M. *How to Do It: Guides to Good Living for Renaissance Italians.* Chicago and London: University of Chicago Press, 1999.

Braudel, Fernand. *Civilization and Capitalism, 15th–18th Century.* 3 volumes. Translated by Siân Reynolds. New York: Harper and Row, 1982.

Bristol, Michael D. *Carnival and Theater: Plebeian Culture and the Structure of Authority in Renaissance England.* New York and London: Routledge, 1985.

Campion, Thomas. *The Works of Thomas Campion.* Edited by Walter R. Davis. New York: Norton, 1970.

Caselli, Giovanni. *The Renaissance and the New World.* New York: Peter Bedrick, 1985.

Darnton, Robert. "Peasants Tell Tales: The Meaning of Mother Goose" in *The Great Cat Massacre and Other Episodes in French Cultural History.* New York: Basic Books, 1984.

Davis, Michael Justin. *The England of William Shakespeare.* New York: Dutton, 1987.

Davis, Natalie Zemon. *The Return of Martin Guerre.* Cambridge, MA: Harvard University Press, 1983.

Denieul-Cormier, Annie. *The Renaissance in France, 1488–1559.* Translated by Anne and Christopher Fremantle. London: George Allen and Unwin, 1969.

Editors of Time-Life Books. *What Life Was Like at the Rebirth of Genius: Renaissance Italy, AD 1400–1550.* Alexandria, VA: Time-Life Books, 1999.

Editors of Time-Life Books. *What Life Was Like in the Realm of Elizabeth: England AD 1533–1603.* Alexandria, VA: Time-Life Books, 1998.

Grendler, Paul F., editor in chief. *Encyclopedia of the Renaissance.* 6 volumes. New York: Charles Scribner's Sons, 1999.

Hale, John. *The Civilization of Europe in the Renaissance.* New York: Touchstone, 1993.

Hoffman, Philip T. *Growth in a Traditional Society: The French Countryside, 1450–1815.* Princeton, NJ: Princeton University Press, 1996.

Huse, Norbert, and Wolfgang Wolters. *The Art of Renaissance Venice: Architecture, Sculpture, and Painting, 1460–1590*. Translated by Edmund Jephcott. Chicago and London: University of Chicago Press, 1990.

Jardine, Lisa. *Worldly Goods: A New History of the Renaissance*. New York: Doubleday, 1996.

Johnson, Paul. *The Renaissance: A Short History*. New York: Modern Library, 2000.

Kelsey, Harry. *Sir Francis Drake: The Queen's Pirate*. New Haven and London: Yale University Press, 1998.

King, Margaret L. *Women of the Renaissance*. Chicago and London: University of Chicago Press, 1991.

Kurlansky, Mark. *Cod: A Biography of the Fish That Changed the World*. New York: Penguin Books, 1997.

Pritchard, R. E., editor. *Shakespeare's England: Life in Elizabethan and Jacobean Times*. Gloucestershire: Sutton Publishing, 1999.

Rabb, Theodore. *Renaissance Lives: Portraits of an Age*. New York: Pantheon, 1993.

Reader's Digest Association. *Everyday Life through the Ages*. London and New York: Reader's Digest Association, 1992.

Roberts, J. M. *The Making of the European Age*. New York: Oxford University Press, 1999.

Rowse, A. L. *The Elizabethan Renaissance: The Life of the Society*. New York: Charles Scribner's Sons, 1971.

Shakespeare, William. *Complete Works, Compact Edition*. Edited by Stanley Wells et al. Oxford: Clarendon Press, 1988.

Singman, Jeffrey L. *Daily Life in Elizabethan England*. Westport, CT: Greenwood Press, 1995.

Strauss, Gerald. *Nuremberg in the Sixteenth Century*. New York: John Wiley, 1966.

Tannahill, Reay. *Food in History*. New York: Stein and Day, 1973.

Wheaton, Barbara Ketcham. *Savoring the Past: The French Kitchen and Table from 1300 to 1789*. New York: Touchstone, 1996.

# SOURCES FOR QUOTATIONS

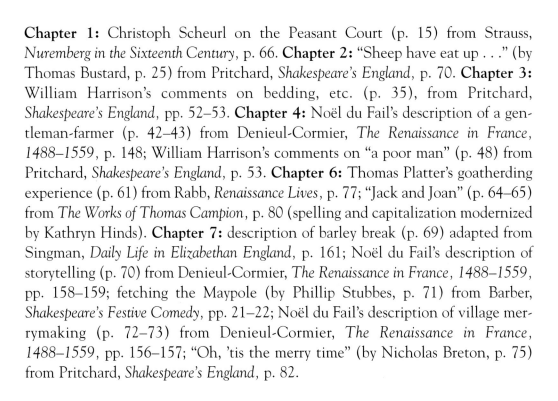

**Chapter 1:** Christoph Scheurl on the Peasant Court (p. 15) from Strauss, *Nuremberg in the Sixteenth Century*, p. 66. **Chapter 2:** "Sheep have eat up . . ." (by Thomas Bustard, p. 25) from Pritchard, *Shakespeare's England*, p. 70. **Chapter 3:** William Harrison's comments on bedding, etc. (p. 35), from Pritchard, *Shakespeare's England*, pp. 52–53. **Chapter 4:** Noël du Fail's description of a gentleman-farmer (p. 42–43) from Denieul-Cormier, *The Renaissance in France, 1488–1559*, p. 148; William Harrison's comments on "a poor man" (p. 48) from Pritchard, *Shakespeare's England*, p. 53. **Chapter 6:** Thomas Platter's goatherding experience (p. 61) from Rabb, *Renaissance Lives*, p. 77; "Jack and Joan" (p. 64–65) from *The Works of Thomas Campion*, p. 80 (spelling and capitalization modernized by Kathryn Hinds). **Chapter 7:** description of barley break (p. 69) adapted from Singman, *Daily Life in Elizabethan England*, p. 161; Noël du Fail's description of storytelling (p. 70) from Denieul-Cormier, *The Renaissance in France, 1488–1559*, pp. 158–159; fetching the Maypole (by Phillip Stubbes, p. 71) from Barber, *Shakespeare's Festive Comedy*, pp. 21–22; Noël du Fail's description of village merrymaking (p. 72–73) from Denieul-Cormier, *The Renaissance in France, 1488–1559*, pp. 156–157; "Oh, 'tis the merry time" (by Nicholas Breton, p. 75) from Pritchard, *Shakespeare's England*, p. 82.

All Shakespeare quotes are from *William Shakespeare, Complete Works, Compact Edition*, edited by Stanley Wells et al. (Oxford: Clarendon Press, 1988).

# INDEX

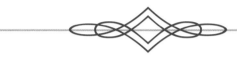

Page numbers for illustrations are in boldface